COWS

LIKE YOU'VE NEVER SEEN

BILLINGS COUNTY PUBLIC SCHOOL
Box 307
Medora, North Dakota 58645

From the Author

I am a full-time farmer by vocation and photographer by avocation. The idea of cows with hats began as a whim. These gentle creatures give so much of themselves, and they seemed to enjoy the antics as much as the photographer. I hope you enjoy the book as much as I did putting it together.

I would like to dedicate this book to Tasha & company; without these gentle and wonderful creatures these photos would not be possible.

I would also like to thank Ann Lundeen, for her supprt and enthusiasm; Sheri Tomhave and Carl Krause for their help and apologies for occasionally putting them in wild situations for some of these photos.

Copyright 2000 by David Lill

Published by
Adventure Publications, Inc.
P.O. Box 269
Cambridge, MN 55008

Printed in China
ISBN 1-885061-83-8

About the Author

David Lill is a bachelor dairy farmer who lives in northern Minnesota near Fergus Falls. Following a whim one day, he put a hat on one of his cows and took her picture. With affection and regard that most people would consider uncommon in his vocation, David continued to photograph his glamour cows. What began as a whim blossomed into a project that enhanced David's relationship with his herd and alters the general view of cows. "These

gentle creatures give so much of themselves," he says, "I thought it was time to have some fun. They seem to enjoy it too."

David Lill explores the possibility that even the most vigorous and demanding lifestyle can be brightened by looking at cows from a different angle...like you've never seen!

(See pages 70-72 for more photos of David with his cows.)

Bad hair day – I can't do a thing with these cowlicks!

We're having chicken.

The Hustler — you gotta know when to hold 'em.

Mother Superior

Any udder requests?

Hay there!
How YOU doin'?

Left at the halter.

Enquiring cows want to know.

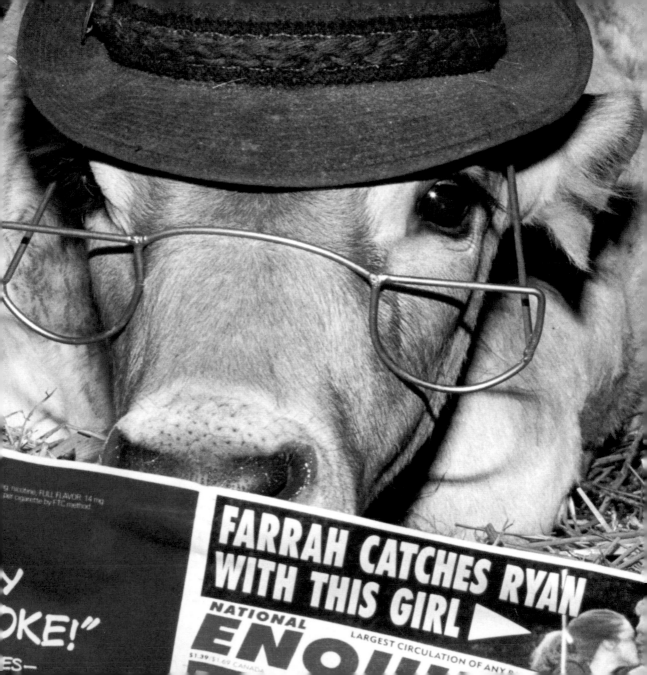

OK, who ate the
refried beans?

He didn't ask you how you feel –
he said you'd make good veal.

Ok son, now about
those cute little heifers
down by the polebarn...

BILLINGS COUNTY PUBLIC SCHOOL
Box 307
Medora, North Dakota 58645

Hooooow-dy!

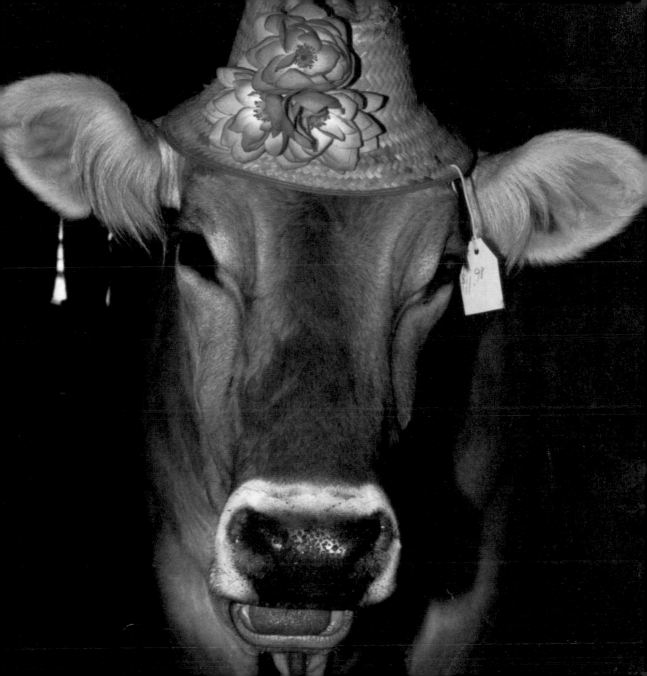

You should see what we
do with cattle rustlers
around these parts!

Tell me your symptoms —
I'm all ears.

She's always putting herself
on a pedestal.

It's so hard to
coordinate accessories —
do you think the boa
is too much?

We need to talk —
I've got a beef with you!

The officer's mess?
Look to my rear.

I'll bet Martha Stewart doesn't make her own fertilizer!

Moodini can make magic for YOU!

Have you seen
my blue suede shoes?
Viva Las Vegas!

I'm not jumping,
and that's my final answer!

Tell me the truth...
who's the cutest here?

Is breakfast ready?

Thank God I got through the swimsuit competition!

Bessie Silver Heels

What are the chances we'd all buy the same hat?

OK, I'm up!
So what's for breakfast?
Milk...again?!

To beef, or not to beef,
that is the question.

Udderly Gothic

Watch the close-ups, hay breath!

A photo op? Where? Wait...
I'll be dressed in a minute!

She loves me,
she loves me not...

Don't cry — you knew your reign had to end!

I'm sorry — you can't keep the crown!

Yes, I love you, too. Now, can I get back in my truck?